PARK COUNTY LIBRARY
SYSTEM
POWELL BRANCH LIBRARY
Powell, Wyoming 82435

This book begins with a flower. The story of Chinese papercuts begins with flowers – flowers that celebrate the newness of spring. We dedicate our book to Wang Tsu-kang and all of the papercut artists whom we met in our travels across China. It is written in appreciation for their good-natured patience as we sat at their elbows watching them design and cut examples of this joyful folk art. We are especially grateful to Wang Tsu-kang, who agreed to let us use some of his papercuts in hopes that his work could improve the friendship and understanding of the Chinese and American peoples.

MAKING CHINESE

Published simultaneously in Canada by
General Publishing, Limited, Toronto.

10 9 8 7 6 5 4 3 2

Robert and Corinne Borja

PAPERCUTS

Albert Whitman & Company, Chicago

China has long used the dragon as its symbol. This papercut is an enlarged version of a design from Zhejiang Province. A scissorcut. *(1) Numbers following some captions refer to locations on the map on pages 38-39.*

How do the Chinese fill their homes with flowers all year long? With some paper and a pair of scissors or a knife everything is possible. In this book you will find out why the Chinese papercut is so special and how it is made. You will learn how papercuts were used in the past and how they are used today. You will take scissors in hand and make papercuts yourself. Along the way we will show you papercuts from many different places in China. Welcome to the way of Chinese papercuts!

CONTENTS

WHAT IS A PAPERCUT?

A papercut is a design or picture cut out of paper. Some are big simple shapes cut with scissors. Others are lacy designs cut with a knife.

The Chinese are masters of the art of papercutting. Most Chinese papercuts, such as the one of magpies and plum blossoms on the next page, are decorative designs. They look best with light coming from behind them. Then all the lines are sharp and clear. Everything looks lively—the flowers shine, the birds arch and sing.

Other papercuts are of landscapes or people. Often cuts are designed and painted so they do not look flat. In the papercut on this page, pavilions are behind trees, and boats sail on a river behind the pavilions. The cut has been painted with delicate colors, giving the shapes a soft look.

Some papercuts are made for a special occasion and then thrown away. Others are so beautiful they are kept as works of art. One day you may be so skilled that your papercuts will be works of art, too. Then you will be a master papercutter.

Left: Subtle hand coloring creates the effect of the misty hills and the Li Jiang River in this design from the city of Guilin. A knifecut. ***(2)***

Right: This modern cut is of a traditional subject, magpies and plum blossoms. The word for magpies is *si.* It also means "happiness." Red stands for joy and life. A knifecut.

THE CUTTING

Have you ever cut a design out of paper? If so, you know that all the parts must remain connected or the cut will fall apart.

Look closely at the papercuts in this book. Can you tell which cuts have been made with a knife and which with scissors?

The fantastic bird above, called a phoenix, was cut for us in China by a master papercutter, Wang Tsu-kang. He used scissors and strong paper. Often many papercuts are cut at once, but Wang Tsu-kang made only one. He did not draw the phoenix first or use a pattern, as is usually done. He has made so many papercuts that he can see a design on paper exactly as if it were drawn there. He cut out the bird in one continuing motion, never stopping to go back.

Chinese scissors, such as the ones Wang Tsu-kang used, have large handles and short blades. They allow the papercutter to use his

Above: The phoenix is a symbol for southern China. This graceful design from Shanghai is cut in white. Notice how the three arched feathers in the comb repeat in the tail. A scissorcut. ***(3)***

Right: An interesting pattern of dark and light characterizes this cut from the city of Hangzhou, famous for its willow trees and gardens. A knifecut. ***(4)***

The Chinese papercut knife. A knifecut.

whole hand with very little effort. (See the papercut of Chinese scissors on page 4.)

The scene on this page was cut with a knife. The Chinese papercutting knife has a long point that can be sharpened on both edges. Some knives have curved blades for making curved cutouts, and some have punches for making circles. Handles are narrow so that the knife can be easily turned in the hand.

The landscape below is one of a number of cuts that were made at the same time. Thin sheets of paper were stacked and fastened to a board. A drawing was mounted on top of the sheets. Then a young woman cut down through the drawing and all the paper.

To make the round cutouts for the flowers, the artist made one tiny cut after another. See the small notches in the circles? Sharp corners like these are often found in knifecuts.

THE PAPER

Paper is terrific stuff. It can be thin as tissue or thick as cardboard. It can be folded and cut into different shapes. Paper comes in many colors, and, if we like, we can put more color on it. Unlike cloth, paper doesn't go out of shape or fray when it is cut. It is usually cheap and easy to get.

Paper is versatile and obedient. The Chinese word *yin* is a good word to describe paper. *Yin* means "to be accepting." Paper is ready to be made into something; it easily accepts another form.

Paper is matted vegetable fiber that has been dried and pressed. To make paper, plant fibers such as wood or cotton are chopped and cooked into soft pulp; then the fibers are passed over a screen on which they mat together into a sheet. The sheet is squeezed, dried, and pressed until it becomes thin and smooth.

In China there are stores that sell nothing but paper, including brilliantly colored varieties that make fine papercuts. People also hand color their own paper using dyes and wide brushes.

The first paper came from China about two thousand years ago. How did the Chinese think of it? Here's our guess.

At some time people must have noticed the way animal hairs mat together. They eventually matted hairs together themselves to make robes and to cover their tents. We call this material *felt*. Then a clever fellow named Ts'ai Lun matted together fibers from the bark of the mulberry tree. When the matted fibers were dried, smoothed, and pressed, he had a material that could be folded, cut, and written upon. Ts'ai Lun had invented paper.

There are many beautiful kinds of paper to use for papercuts. Look in a dime store or grocery store for different kinds of colored paper. If you go to an art store, ask to see Pantone papers, Japanese origami papers, pastel papers, or shiny metallic papers.

This knifecut of thin, absorbent *hsuan* paper is one of many cut at the same time. The papercuts were hand colored by letting dyes run down through the stack of sheets. The figure, designed by Wang Lao-shan, is a character from the Peking Opera.

PAPERCUTS IN CHINA'S PAST

When holidays roll around, we want to spread our good feelings and excitement by decorating things around us. We want to fill our ordinary, plain world with bright, fresh colors and shapes. Holidays are a good time to make papercuts.

This is what the Chinese have done for about nineteen hundred years. In ancient times the papercutter for the emperor made

There are many papercut designs of roosters. This bold knifecut is from the mountainous province of Shaanxi. Notice the cut-out circles, the long curving slits, the areas with one curved and one straight side or one toothed and one smooth side. These are favorite patterns for knifecuts. ***(5)***

papercuts to please his ruler. The emperor would give his guests these special papercuts at the New Year's festivities.

But it was not necessary to be an emperor to have papercuts. The common people had paper, too, and soon it became popular for everyone to decorate with papercuts on special occasions. The working people were not trained artists, but they had an eye for beauty, anyway. With bits of colored paper and a kitchen knife or sewing scissors, flowers could bloom in their homes. They called the papercuts *huang hua,* "window flowers."

Some men became very skilled at papercutting. Such a skilled person was called a master. The master's whole family would help make his papercuts. The master created his own style, developing special tools for

This deer is an enlargement of a detail from a complex papercut. Animals are often pictured decorated with flowers. The heads are most often seen from the side, in profile. A scissorcut.

Ideas for designs come from what we see around us. Views such as this of Piled Silk Hill in Guangsi Juang Autonomous Region in southern China have inspired many great paintings. The paintings, in turn, have inspired papercuts.

People live close to nature in China. They rise at dawn and do slow, graceful morning exercises, called *tai ji quan,* in a serene outdoor setting such as this place on the island of Gushan, in the city of Hangzhou. It is not surprising that most papercuts are of animals, flowers, and other natural subjects.

punching out holes and curves of different shapes. The best designs were passed down from generation to generation within a family. Often a village or region would become famous for a certain kind of papercut.

The most special time of the year in China is New Year's. Then the Chinese remind themselves that although the earth seems cold and dead, spring will soon come and life will begin again. New Year's is a time for making resolutions, a time for making all things new.

Until recently, most windows in Chinese homes were made of tough paper instead of glass. New Year's was the time to replace the window paper. On the new paper would be glued fresh window flowers, to be enjoyed from the inside during the day and from the outside at night. Paper that covered the walls was replaced, too, and bright new papercuts were put on the fresh walls.

Large papercuts were pasted on the ceiling; papercuts decorated mirrors. Papercuts also decorated the pictures of the gods of health, wealth, and long life that were put up outside near the front door.

Left: Chinese papercuts sometimes reflect the lines of graceful buildings as well as the lines of nature.

A scissorcut embroidery pattern, perhaps used to decorate a neckline. The design is from Jiangxi Province, an area known for its needlework. *(6)*

CHINESE PAPERCUTS TODAY

Today papercuts remain an important part of the Chinese New Year's celebration. Papercuts decorate houses; they appear on presents and lanterns; they fly like tiny flags atop cakes and other dishes. Papercuts are used for birthdays, weddings, and other special days, too. On national holidays the streets are aglow with paper decorations, including streamers covered with papercut *calligraphy,* or writing, wishing all well.

Many papercuts were used for good luck in the old days. One design was supposed to bring rain, another protect against fire. Cuts were displayed in hopes of bringing health, wealth, or a new baby into a family.

Papercuts have always been used as embroidery patterns. The flower above and the small figure at the right are examples of this kind of design. A papercut is pasted on cloth,

A strong, simple knifecut by the artist Mu Kwei-ying. The design is based on a character from a play about a brave woman. The character is often used in shadow plays on holidays.

From the desert in Shanxi Province comes this knifecut design of a proud camel. Notice how the hair has been cut; sharp points like these are often found on knifecuts. *(7)*

then stitched over until the pattern is covered.

Papercuts are used in the technique called *stencilling*. A design is cut from heavy waterproof paper, then color is brushed through the cutout areas onto cloth. Papercuts make good shadow puppets, too. The cutouts are mounted on sticks and held before a lighted screen.

A scissorcut for embroidery. The child is Lui Hai, a "bringer of good fortune." The round shapes represent old Chinese coins, which had square holes to string them together.

SUBJECTS, NEW AND OLD

The first papercuts were tiny flowers of gold and other bright colors, displayed to welcome spring. Soon papercut designs developed symbolic meaning. The plum blossom, chrysanthemum, pine, and bamboo designs represented the human spirit. The lion and the dragon stood for courage. The peach, crane, and turtle symbolized long life; fishes stood for wealth. The lotus blossom, pig, and pomegranate were believed to bring children.

For a long time birds and flowers were a popular subject for papercuts. About fifteen hundred years ago artists began painting birds and flowers, and soon these paintings inspired papercut designers.

For years papercutters have designed cuts after characters in the ever-popular Peking Opera, famous for its colorful costumes.

Modern papercuts focus on contemporary ideas. One design proclaiming the equality of women has the title "Women Hold Up Half the Sky." Many modern cuts have political themes.

Above: A delicate knifecut of a popular traditional subject, a bird with flowers.

Right: A modern knifecut from the city of Foshan. The scene is from a story about the Young Pioneers, a Chinese youth group. The Young Pioneers are shown climbing a mountain in pursuit of an enemy of the people. Traditional patterns are used for the leaves and flowers, but the composition of open and solid areas is modern. ***(8)***

LET'S MAKE A PAPERCUT

Are you ready to try your own papercut? Here's what you'll need to make a cut of the bird on the facing page.

- A piece of thin, see-through paper, such as tracing paper.
- A piece of brightly colored paper that is not too thick. You might use Pantone paper or origami.
- A medium-sized pair of scissors with thin blades.
- A good white glue, such as Elmer's.
- A pencil.

Use the thin paper and a pencil to trace the bird. This tracing will be your pattern. On the back of the pattern put small dots of glue just outside the drawing and inside the eye and wingline. Be careful not to get glue inside the outline of the bird.

Press the tracing onto the colored paper and let it dry firmly in position. As you cut, the tracing paper will fall away.

Work slowly and follow the directions as closely as you can. When you have had some practice, you will be able to cut more freely and quickly.

1. Following the pattern, cut along the top of the beak toward the head. Keep the scissors in place. Turn the paper and cut the top of the head.

2. Open the scissors and place them back in the cut. Turn the paper in the direction of the tail and cut in long strokes, continuing past the end of the tail.

3. Turn the paper around and cut the underside of the tail. Remove the scissors. Make a preliminary cut across the bottom of the feathers. Cut up both sides of each feather.

4. Remove the scissors and cut just to the tip of the shortest toe. Then cut along the flat "leg" toward the tail. Turn the paper and cut up to where the shortest tail feather begins. Remove the scissors. Make a preliminary cross-cut close to the tips of the toes; then make cuts to separate the toes.

5. Cut toward the head along the curve of the breast. Open your scissors again when the line changes direction and continue cutting past the end of the beak.

6. To make the eye, cut between the upper and lower parts of the beak. Continue into the head and cut out a small oval.

7. Where the back joins the head, cut a curve into the body. Remove the scissors. Make a second cut alongside the first one, tapering to a point at the inside end of the curve.

You have completed your first Chinese papercut!

This lark is a detail from an elaborate scissorcut from Jiangsu Province. Like most papercuts from southern China, it is almost all curves. *(9)*

Right: For each papercut design, a drawing is made first. Here an artist adds some finishing touches.

Far right: Knifecuts are usually made by holding the knife vertically and pushing it straight down into a stack of thin papers. The papers are fastened to a specially prepared board.

SOME HELPFUL HINTS

Chinese master papercutters are very skilled at using scissors. Here are some hints that will help improve your own techniques.

As you cut, keep your two hands close together. One hand holds the paper, the other uses the scissors. For better control, try resting the bottom scissor blade on the fingertips of the hand holding the paper.

Open your scissors wide and make as long a cut as possible in one stroke. But don't try to close the blades all the way unless they are very pointed.

When you cannot complete a cut in one stroke, look ahead for a fairly straight place to stop and begin again. Reopen the blades and place them all the way back into the cut. Do not turn the paper until you begin cutting again. Look where you restarted. Is a little point sticking out? If so, you did not place the scissors all the way back into the cut. Does the cut change direction too sharply? You probably turned the paper before you started to cut.

Be careful that you do not cut too deeply into a design. You may weaken or cut off something you wish to keep.

Never go back to fix something up. The fix-up always shows. Do your best, and if your papercut isn't just the way you want it, try another one.

Master Wang Tsu-kang cuts a scissorcut, his specialty. He prefers to stand, with light coming from his left.

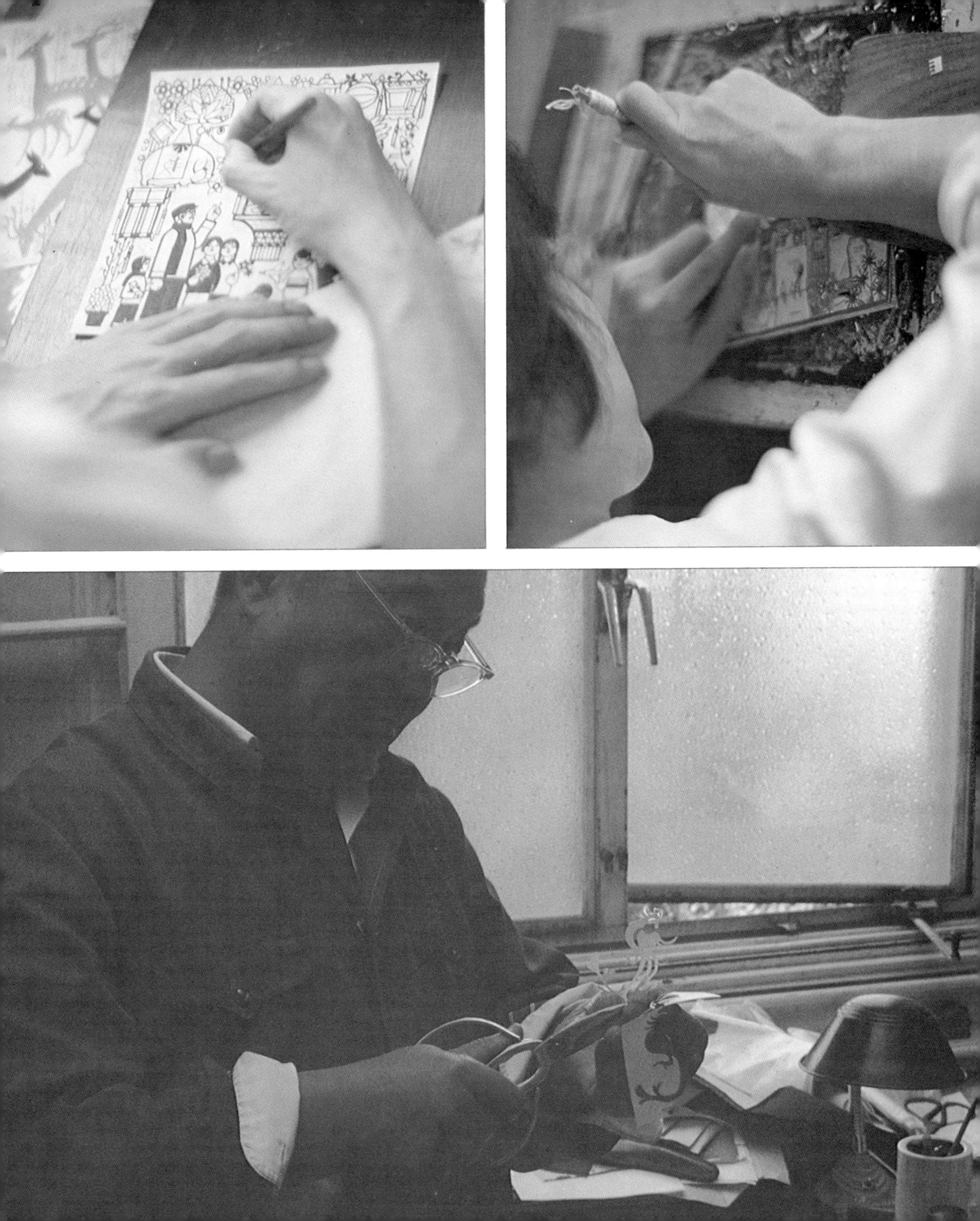

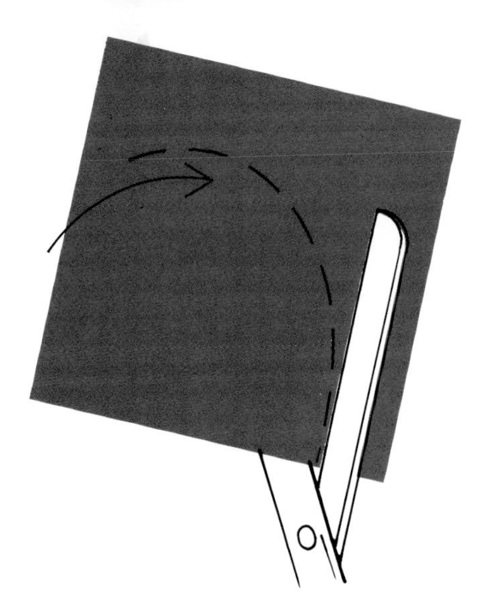

1. Chinese papercuts are mostly curves. To make smooth curves, keep your scissors pointing in the same direction and turn the paper, not the scissors, as you cut. Tilt the blades a bit to the side.

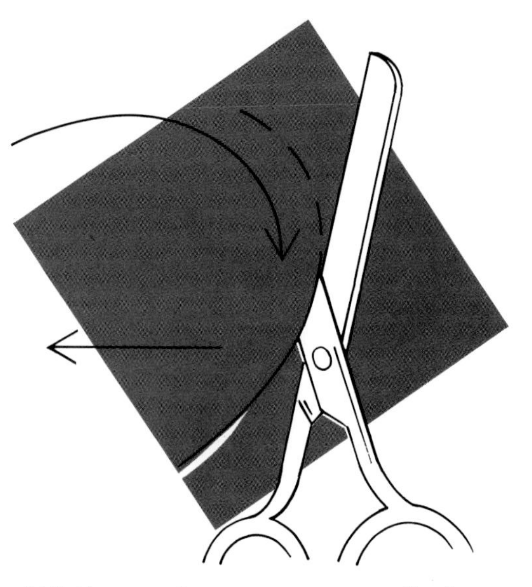

2. While cutting a curve, pull the paper sideways very gently. This will give you better control.

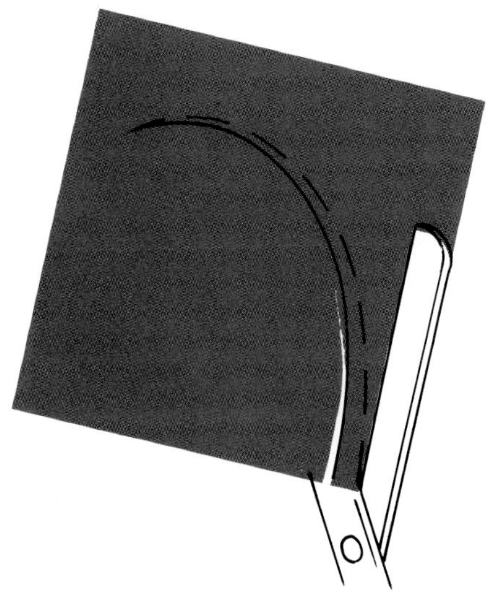

3. To cut a slit, you should cut the left side first if you are right-handed. Then the blades of the scissors won't be in the way when you cut the other side.

4. If you are left-handed, cut the right side of the slit first.

CUTTING A FLOWER

Here's an easy way to cut out the more elaborate design on this page.

Make a pattern by tracing half of the flower (just to the broken line) on see-through paper. Place dots of glue on the pattern outside the design and inside the cutout areas.

Fold in half a piece of colored paper that is slightly bigger than the flower. Glue the outer edges of the paper together to help hold the two sides in position. Glue the pattern to the colored paper so that the center of the flower runs along the fold.

Cut away the inside areas of the design. Then cut the outside edge. Try to make the curves smooth. Be careful not to cut off the narrow stem!

A PICTURE WITH A BORDER

Trace the flower on the opposite page onto thin paper and glue the pattern to colored paper. Beginning at the stem, try to cut out the whole flower without taking your scissors out of the paper. Cut down between the petals, then turn the paper around and cut back out. To make the sharp points in the center of the flower, cut just past each point before beginning the next curve.

For the background, you'll need tracing paper and colored paper about eight inches wide and seven inches high. Fold the colored paper in half from top to bottom and from side to side. Make a tracing of one-fourth of the border and put dots of glue on the areas that will be cut out. Glue the pattern to the folded paper, with the cutout design near the unfolded edges.

Cut out the design through all four layers of paper. When you unfold the paper, you will have the completed border design. Press the folds flat with a warm iron. Glue your flower to the center.

Try tracing and cutting other scissorcuts in this book. Begin with the large, simple designs. You might want to make borders for some of your papercuts.

This is a detail from a design made to be cut with scissors. From the city of Nanjing. *(10)*

DESIGN YOUR OWN PAPERCUTS

Here's how you can design your own papercuts.

Look around for things with interesting shapes—trees, flowers, buildings. When you find a subject you like, study it with the light coming from behind it. Can you imagine your subject as a papercut against a window? Does it have interesting lines and curves? Can you recognize it from its outside shape?

When you have found a good subject, make a drawing to use for a pattern.

Use a black felt marker to roughly fill in the general shape, then add the fine details with the tip of the marker or a pencil. Use a pencil to indicate areas that will be cut out of the middle. The shiny lead will show against the dull black.

When you are satisfied with your pattern, glue it to colored paper and cut out the design. Remember that inside cutout areas are made by working in from the outside edge, just as you cut the bird's eye using the design on page 20 or the center of the flower in the design on page 27.

You might try cutting some designs out of white paper, then mounting the white papercuts on deep-colored background paper.

A STAINED GLASS DESIGN

In China many papercut designs are pasted over printed pictures. The banner at the left has a gold cutout design pasted over a picture, creating a stained-glass effect. You can make a similar design to put over a photograph or a picture from a magazine.

Place tracing paper over a picture you like and draw lines around interesting objects or areas you wish to emphasize. Make a border around the outside edge and add a design at the top or bottom. Use a felt marker to thicken the lines.

Glue this pattern to colored paper and cut out the design. Carefully place the papercut over the picture; then glue the cut in position.

You might use this technique to make a bookmark or a poster or to highlight a favorite photograph of someone in your family.

If you do not wish to glue the cut to the photo, cover it with a piece of clear plastic and glue the cut to the plastic.

MORE THAN ONE

The Chinese often make more than one papercut at a time. To make a small number of cuts, a design is sewn on top of several pieces of paper. Then the design and the papers are cut all at once with scissors or placed on a board and cut with a knife.

To make a greater number of cuts, a stack of papers is positioned on a smooth board and nailed down or fastened into place with a wooden frame. Then a knife is used to cut down through the pattern and all the paper.

An easy way for you to make several papercuts at once is to staple a few pieces of thin paper together with the design on top. Use strong scissors to cut through all the paper at once.

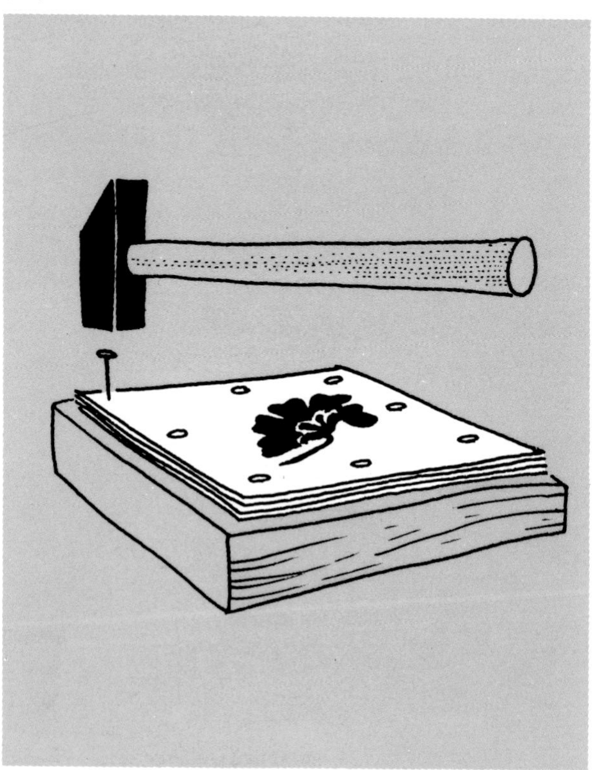

You can also use glue to hold two or three sheets of thin paper together. Glue the pattern onto the first sheet, then hold the pattern and first sheet up to a window, pressing the pattern against the window. The damp glue spots will show through the colored paper enough so you can add more glue to the back, matching the spots, and then glue another sheet onto it. If your paper is thin enough, you can add several more sheets in this manner.

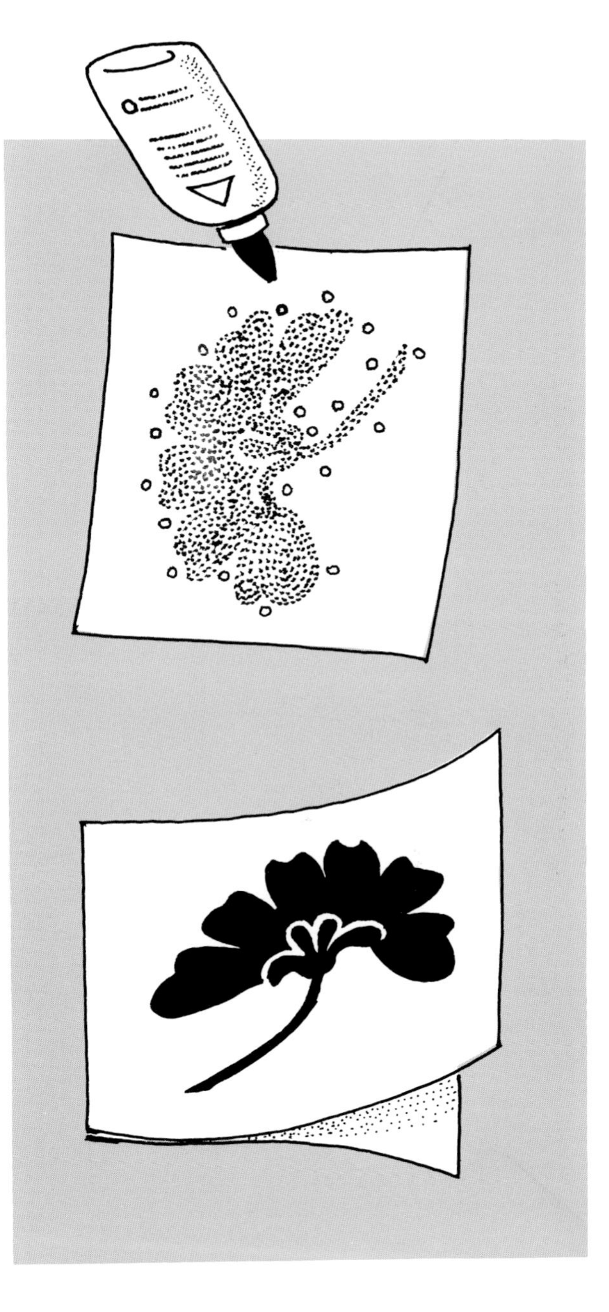

HAND COLORING

Colored inks and/or transparent watercolors are bright and beautiful for coloring papercuts.

"Sharp (*chien*) and bright (*yang*)" is the rule for colors used in Chinese folk arts!

The Chinese use beautiful dyes and watercolors to make multicolored papercuts. Often a stack of cuts is colored all at once. Paint or dye is applied to the top of the stack and allowed to soak down through all the papers. The Chinese use an absorbent paper called *hsuan* for this technique. Japanese mulberry paper, often called rice paper, can also be used.

Try coloring some of your own papercuts. You might begin with the dragon on pages 2 and 3 of this book. Trace the design on thin paper and glue the pattern to medium-weight white paper.

Carefully cut out the dragon and place it on some newspaper. Use watercolors to paint the cut any way that pleases you. To keep the colors bright and clear, remember to clean your brush before you change paints.

Wang Lao-shan designed this beautifully colored cut of a character from the Peking Opera. The addition of color defining the features and clothing completes the design. A knifecut.

This butterfly is a dazzling new scissorcut design from the Shanghai Arts and Crafts Research Institute. ***(11)***

A goldfish design from the Foshan Craft Workshop. A knifecut. ***(12)***

WAYS TO USE YOUR PAPERCUTS

There are many ways to use your papercuts. You might put them in the window as "window flowers." Glue the cut directly to the glass or put it in an envelope made of clear acetate and hang it from the top of the window frame with fishline.

Papercuts make attractive gift-wrap decorations and greeting cards. For mounting finely cut designs, glue and press down one edge first. Turn the cut back. Working out from the glued edge, gradually add more glue to the cut and press the rest of the design carefully into position.

You might want to frame some papercuts. Cut a mat of stiff colored paper to fit a frame. This will be the background for the papercut. Then cut another piece of paper the same size

A rooster scissorcut by Wang Tsu-kang. ***(13)***

A woman tending geese. This knifecut is from a new design series showing women at work.

as the mat. Center your papercut on this paper, in the exact position you want it to be in the frame. Apply glue to the cut. Press the mat facedown onto the cut and the other piece of paper. Turn the mat over, and your design will be pasted in position, ready for the frame.

Papercuts also look fine glued to the front of a clear plastic box or a deep plastic frame. The space behind the cut makes it seem to float.

You can make papercuts out of adhesive-backed vinyl for use on lampshades, walls, mirrors, and notebook covers. Peel the backing off gradually as you press the cut into place.

Chinese puppets are cut from leather, then colored and mounted on sticks. You can make your own papercut puppets using heavy colored paper. Tape the cutouts onto pencils, rulers, or small sticks.

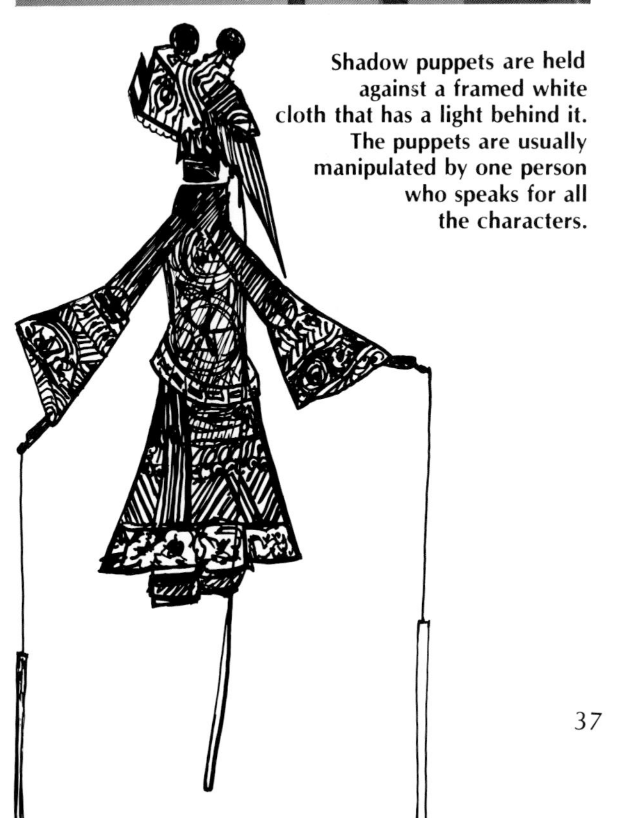

Shadow puppets are held against a framed white cloth that has a light behind it. The puppets are usually manipulated by one person who speaks for all the characters.

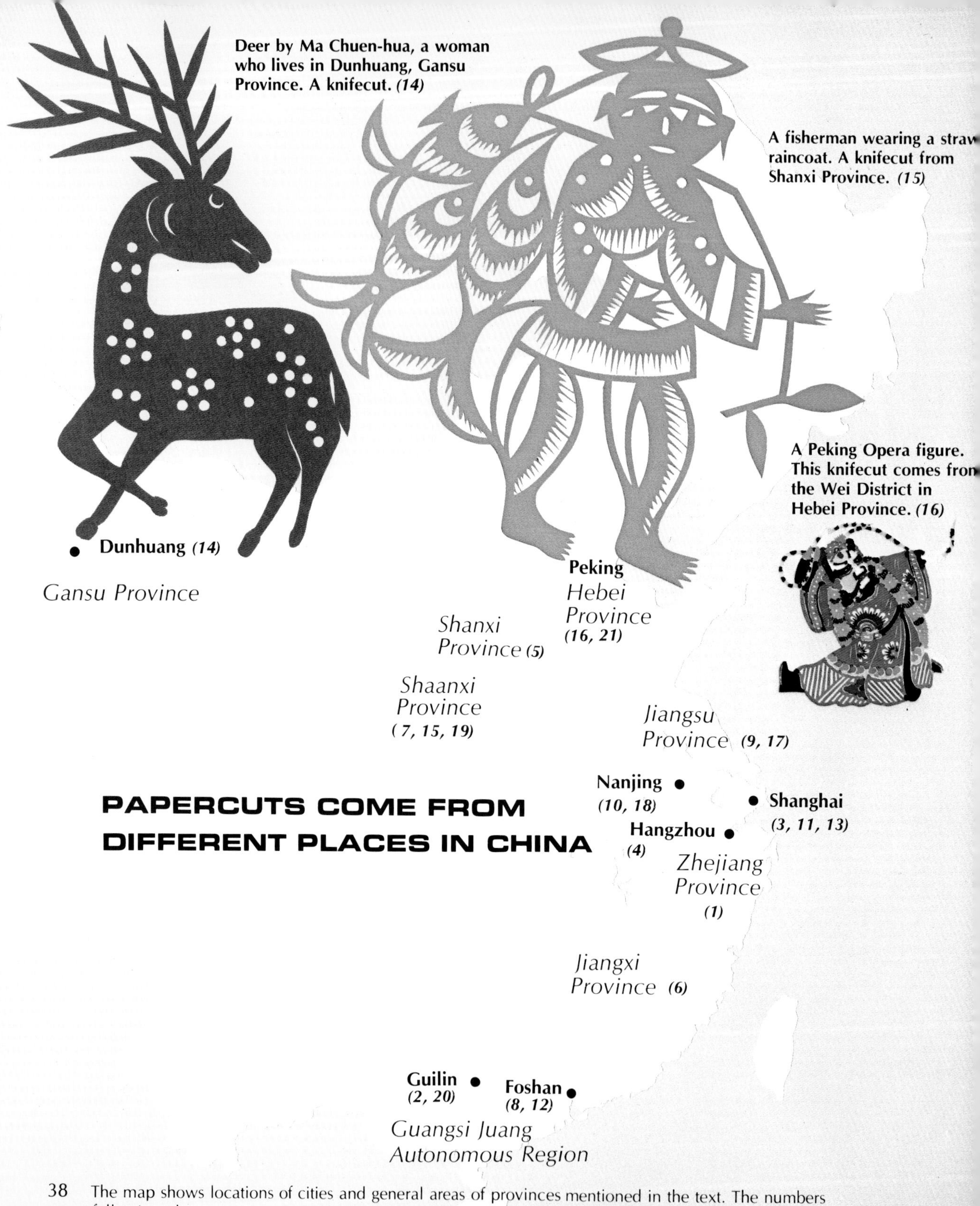

Deer by Ma Chuen-hua, a woman who lives in Dunhuang, Gansu Province. A knifecut. *(14)*

A fisherman wearing a straw raincoat. A knifecut from Shanxi Province. *(15)*

A Peking Opera figure. This knifecut comes from the Wei District in Hebei Province. *(16)*

PAPERCUTS COME FROM DIFFERENT PLACES IN CHINA

The map shows locations of cities and general areas of provinces mentioned in the text. The numbers following place names correspond to numbers given after captions throughout the book.

In spite of their love for horse paintings, the Chinese have few papercuts of horses. This rare example is from Shanxi Province. A knifecut. *(19)*

Also from Jiangsu Province comes this chrysanthemum, designed by Chang Yung-sho. A scissorcut. *(17)*

From Nanjing, Jiangsu Province, comes this framed picture of a popular subject—a man playing his flute atop a water buffalo. A knifecut. *(18)*

A Peking Opera figure from Hebei Province. A knifecut. *(21)*

A knifecut of a scene on the Li Jiang River, in the style of Guilin, Guangsi Juang Autonomous Region. The seals stamped in red identify the cut. *(20)*

A Note from the Authors

After receiving from the Chinese government the first invitation ever extended to a group of artists and designers, we visited China and had the wonderful experience of meeting artists and artisans from all over that country. It was so inspiring to see them apply their skills for our benefit that we wanted to set down some of the things we learned in a book and to share some of the fine papercuts made for us.

This book can be considered a companion to another book of ours, MAKING COLLAGES.

Robert and Corinne Borja.

Note: Except for well-known place names and historical figures, official Pinyin spellings have been used throughout this book.

INDEX

Library of Congress Cataloging in Publication Data
Borja, Robert. Making Chinese papercuts. (Craft books)
SUMMARY: Highlights the origins and uses of Chinese papercutting and presents instructions for many projects, including decorations, greeting cards, and puppets.
1. Paperwork—China—Juvenile literature. [1. Paper work. 2. Handicraft] I. Borja, Corinne, joint author. II. Title. III. Series.
TT870.B653 736'.98 79-18358 ISBN 0-8075-4948-7